W9-BDV-094

ORIGAMI
DECORATIONS AND FLOWERS

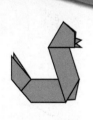

MATTHEW GARDINER

WINDMILL
BOOKS™

New York

Published in 2016 by **Windmill Books,**
an Imprint of Rosen Publishing
29 East 21st Street, New York, NY 10010

Editor: Katie Hewat
Graphic Designer: My Trinh Gardiner
Origami Artists: Darren Scott, Jonathan Baxter, Steven Casey

Cataloging-in-Publication Data
Gardiner, Matthew.
Origami decorations and flowers / by Matthew Gardiner.
p. cm. — (Everything origami)
Includes index.
ISBN 978-1-4777-5627-0 (pbk.)
ISBN 978-1-4777-5626-3 (6 pack)
ISBN 978-1-4777-5550-1 (library binding)
1. Origami — Juvenile literature. 2. Flowers in art — Juvenile literature. I. Title.
TT870.G373 2016
736'.982—d23

Manufactured in the United States of America
CPSIA Compliance Information: Batch # WS15WM: For Further Information contact Rosen Publishing, New York, New York at 1-800-237-9932

CONTENTS

Symbols

Lines

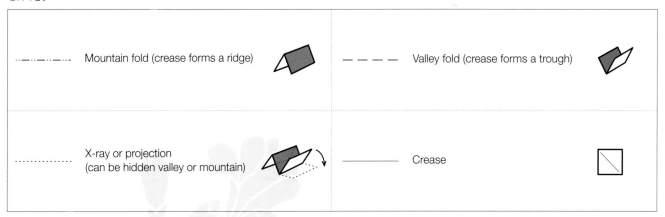

····–··–··–·· Mountain fold (crease forms a ridge)

– – – – – Valley fold (crease forms a trough)

··············· X-ray or projection
(can be hidden valley or mountain)

———— Crease

Arrows

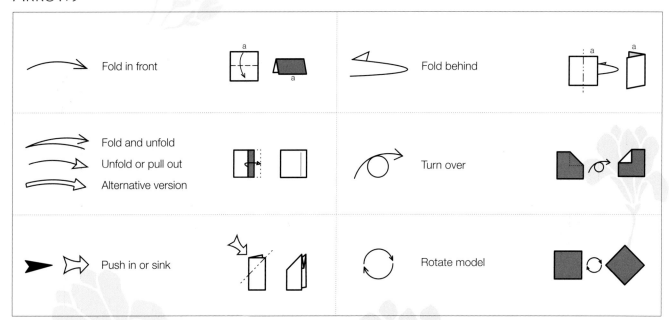

Fold in front

Fold behind

Fold and unfold

Unfold or pull out

Alternative version

Turn over

Push in or sink

Rotate model

Extras

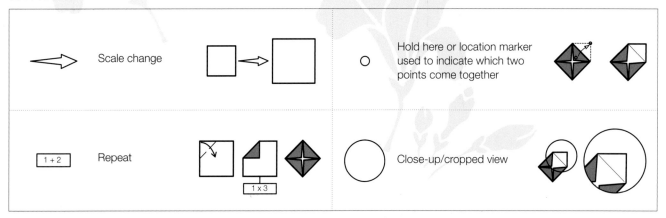

Scale change

O Hold here or location marker
used to indicate which two
points come together

1 + 2 Repeat

Close-up/cropped view

4

TYPES OF FOLDS

BOOK FOLD

Valley fold one edge to another, like closing a book.

CUPBOARD FOLD

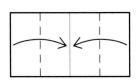

Fold both edges to the middle crease, like closing two cupboard doors.

BLINTZ

Fold all corners to the middle. This was named after a style of pastry called a blintz.

PLEAT

A mountain and valley fold combination.

BISECT –

DIVIDE A POINT IN TWO

Many folds use a corner and two edges to position the fold line. The most common is a bisection, or division of an angle in two.

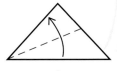

Fold one edge to meet the other, making sure the crease goes through the corner.

INSIDE REVERSE FOLD

The spine of the existing fold is reversed and pushed inside.

OUTSIDE REVERSE FOLD

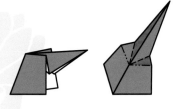

The spine of the existing fold is reversed and wrapped outside.

DOUBLE REVERSE

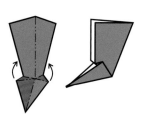

A double reverse fold is two reverse folds made in sequence on the same point.

The last diagram shows the paper slightly unfolded, to illustrate the folds that are made.

INSIDE CRIMP   OUTSIDE CRIMP

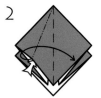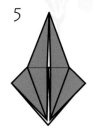

Crimps are often used for making feet or shaping legs. They can be thought of as a pleat mirrored on both sides of the point.

An inside crimp tucks the pleat on the inside of the point.

An outside crimp wraps the pleat over the outside of the point.

PETAL FOLD   The petal fold is found in the bird and lily base.

1	2	3	4	5
Fold top layer to the center crease.	Fold and unfold the top triangle down. Unfold flaps.	Lift the top layer upwards.	Step 3 in progress, the model is 3D. Fold the top layer inwards on existing creases.	Completed petal fold.

SQUASH   A squash fold is the symmetrical flattening of a point. The flattening movement is known as squashing the point.

1	2	3	4
Pre-crease on the line for the squash fold.	Open up the paper by inserting your finger. Fold the paper across.	As you put the paper in place, gently squash the point into a symmetrical shape.	Completed squash fold.

Open Sink

1
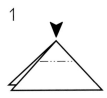

2

3

Pre-crease through all layers along the sink line. It's best to make a mountain and a valley fold on this line.

Open out the point, and push the point into the paper. Take care to reverse folds as shown. The sink should squash flat.

Completed sink.

Rabbit Ear
The rabbit ear fold is named after a most useful shape – that of a rabbit ear. It is used to make a new point.

1

2

3

4

5

6

1- 3. Divide each corner of the triangle with valley folds.

Fold top edges to the bottom, the middle crease will form a point.

Fold the point to one side.

Completed rabbit ear.

Double Rabbit Ear
The double rabbit ear is a rabbit ear fold that is mirrored on both sides of the point.

1
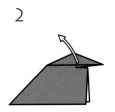

2
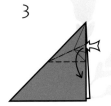

3

4
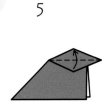

5

6

Make a rabbit ear fold on the point.

Unfold the rabbit ear.

Squash fold the point.

Inside reverse fold the two points.

Valley fold point upwards.

Completed double rabbit ear.

Swivel Fold

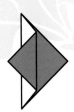

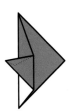

A swivel fold is often made on a pleat. It narrows its two points, and the excess paper swivels under one of the points.

CHOPSTICK DUCK

The chopstick duck is a simple origami model made from a chopstick paper wrapping. This decorative little duck also becomes a rest for your chopsticks for the duration of your meal. You may find it necessary to trim your wrapper at the end, as wrappers come in different dimensions.

A chopstick rest in Japan is called a hashi-oki; they are usually made from ceramic.

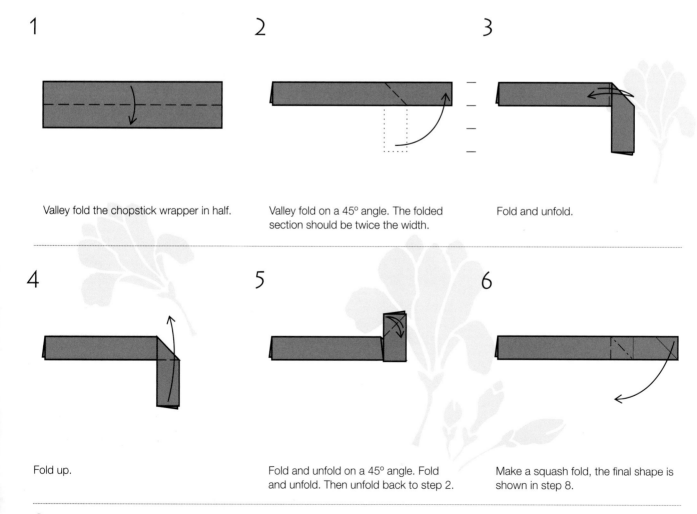

1

Valley fold the chopstick wrapper in half.

2

Valley fold on a 45° angle. The folded section should be twice the width.

3

Fold and unfold.

4

Fold up.

5

Fold and unfold on a 45° angle. Fold and unfold. Then unfold back to step 2.

6

Make a squash fold, the final shape is shown in step 8.

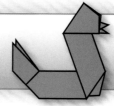

7

The squash fold in progress.

8

Fold up.

9

Fold to the side.

10

Make an inside reverse fold.

11

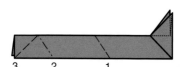

Completed inside reverse fold. Make three folds in order to shape the duck's neck and head.

12

The shaped duck. Unfold back to previous step. If your paper is too long, this is the best time to trim it.

13

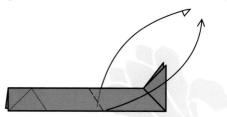

Make an outside reverse fold on the first fold.

14

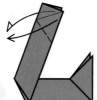

Make an outside reverse fold on the second fold.

15

The model should look like this. The following steps are a close-up of the head.

9

16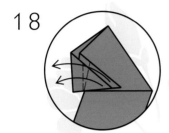

Make an inside reverse fold.

17

Valley fold both points of the beak.

18

Valley fold the points of the beak, fold one higher than the other.

19

Completed step 18. Turn over.

20

This is the duck's "good side."

21

Open the tail on the crease shown.

22

Fold corners to the middle.

23

Fold back to original position. Open the front of the duck slightly with your finger.

24

Completed chopstick duck.

Spanish Box

The traditional Spanish box was brought to the world origami stage by the British magician and origami expert Robert Harbin during his famous BBC television series. It's a practical decorative model, and if you use a 12-inch (30 cm) sheet, or larger, of stiff card you can create a strong vessel for sweets and foods at parties.

The Spanish box is so named because of the decorative pleating on the rim of the box.

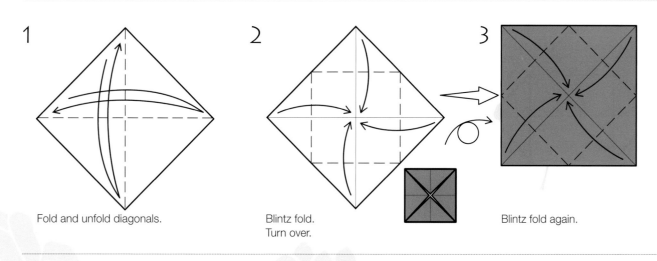

1

Fold and unfold diagonals.

2

Blintz fold.
Turn over.

3

Blintz fold again.

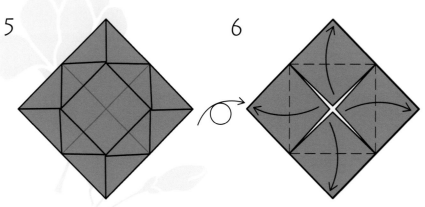

4

Fold top layers from the center to corners.

5

Completed step 4. Turn over.

6

Fold top layers from the center to corners.

7

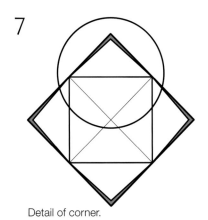

Detail of corner.

8

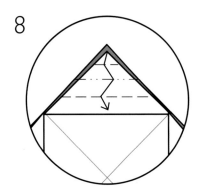

Fold over as shown.

9

Completed step 8.

10

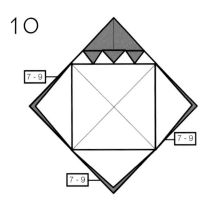

7 - 9

7 - 9

7 - 9

Repeat steps 7-9 on other three corners.

11

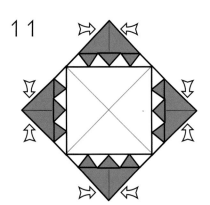

Pinch each corner as shown by
the white arrows making the box 3D.

12

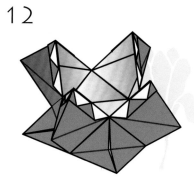

Completed Spanish box.

WENTWORTH DISH

Nick Robinson has a penchant for creating simple paper dishes that have elegant forms and equally elegant paper locks. A paper lock is a sequence of folds that when completed is hard to open, hence the term "lock." The finished shape of his Wentworth dish has variations that can be achieved by altering the angle of one fold.

The dishes Nick Robinson is so fond of folding are inspired by the work of origami artist Philip Shen.

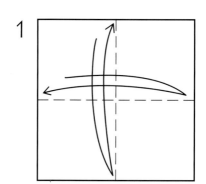

1 Fold and unfold.

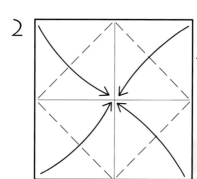

2 Blintz fold. Turn over.
Rotate the paper 45°.

3 Fold and unfold edges to the center as shown. Turn over.

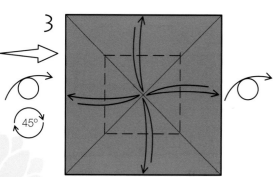

4 Fold corners inside.
Turn over again.

5 Fold and unfold.

6 Fold and unfold.

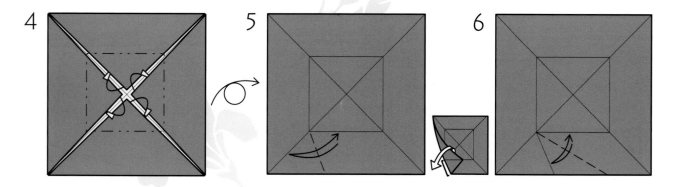

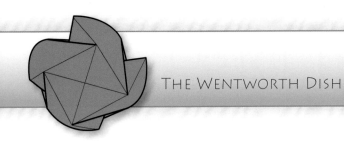

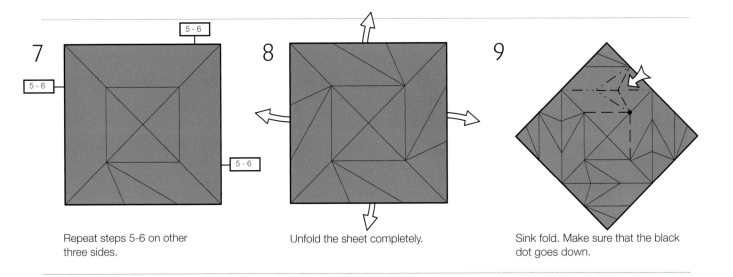

7

8

9

Repeat steps 5-6 on other three sides.

Unfold the sheet completely.

Sink fold. Make sure that the black dot goes down.

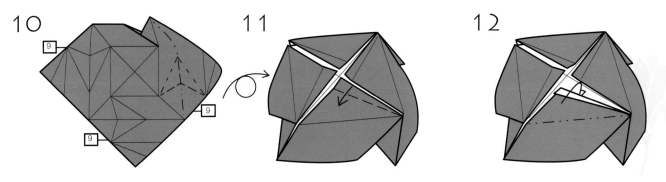

10

11

12

Repeat step 9 on the other three sides. Turn over.

To lock the bottom fold up.

Tuck flap inside for a white center.

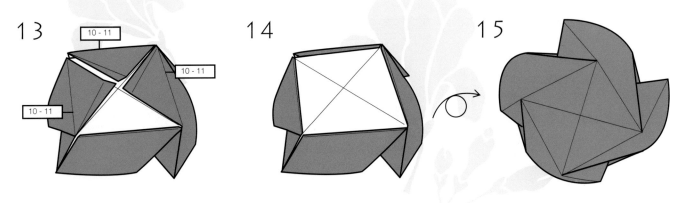

13

14

15

Repeat steps 10-11 on other three sides.

Completed back. Turn over.

Completed dish.

Variation 1

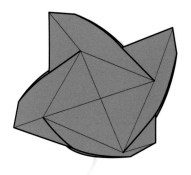

What if we alter this distance?

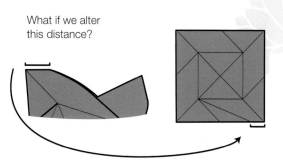

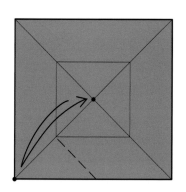

Start from step 6 of the completed dish diagram. Fold and unfold.

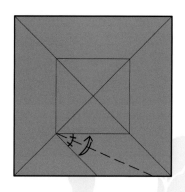

Fold and unfold, bisecting the angle.

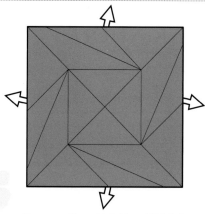

Crease pattern. Unfold and finish from step 9, following completed dish diagram.

Variation 2

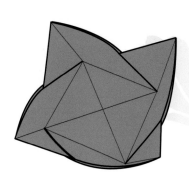

This variation is similar to the previous one, but note the angle of the crease in the second step.

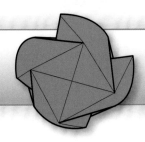

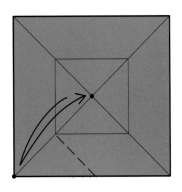

Start from step 6 of the completed dish diagram. Fold and unfold.

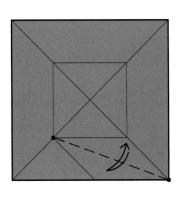

Fold and unfold, corner to corner.

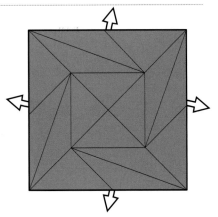

Unfold and finish from step 9 of the dish diagram.

VARIATION 3

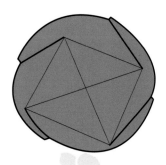

This variation produces a square side profile. The top of the dish can be curved as shown or made angular with strong creases.

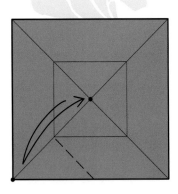

Start from step 6 of the completed dish diagram. Fold and unfold.

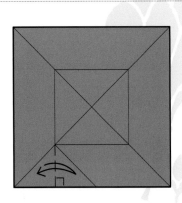

Fold and unfold.

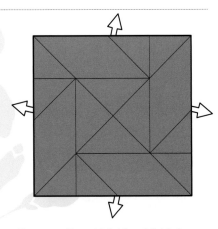

Crease pattern. Unfold and finish from step 9, following completed dish diagram.

STANDING FAN

Table decoration is never complete without an origami-inspired napkin fold. The best results are achieved with an ironed napkin. For large napkins, you may find more pleats in step 2 will make a more attractive fan.

The standing fan napkin fold looks elegant on any table setting.

1

Fold in half.

2

1/4   1/2   1/4

Accordion fold.

3

Fold up all layers.

4

To make the stand fold corners of both layers diagonally, tucking them under the accordion folds.

5

Push outwards.

6

Completed standing fan napkin fold.

WATER LILY

The water lily is a beautiful form, invoking the charm of the lily floating on the water.

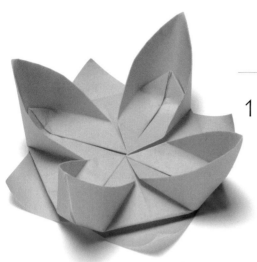

1

Fold and unfold diagonals.

2

Fold corners to the center.

3

Fold corners to the center again.

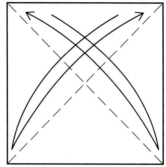

4

Fold indicated corners outwards leaving a small gap at the edges. Turn over.

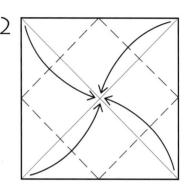

5

While folding the indicated corners to the center, the model will change into 3D.

6

Completed step 5. Turn over.

7

Fold indicated corners outside leaving a little gap at the edges. Turn over.

8

Completed water lily.

IRIS

The iris takes its name from the Greek word for rainbow. Its name reflects the wide range of colors of the iris. This model looks best when folded from a blended or two-toned paper.

The iris is a popular symbol, appearing on the flag of Brussels, and in the fleur-de-lis, the symbol of Florence, Italy.

1

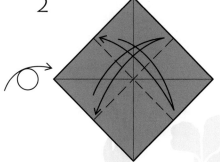

Fold and unfold diagonals. Turn over.

2

Book fold and unfold.

3

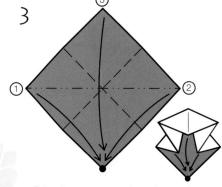

Bring three corners down to meet bottom corner. Start with corners 1 and 2 together followed by corner 3.

4

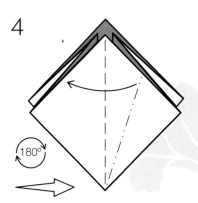

Pre-crease then squash fold.

5

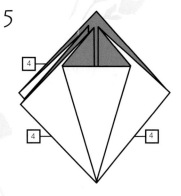

Repeat step 4 on the other three sides.

6

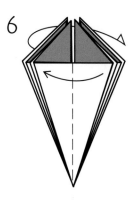

Turn top and back layer over.

7

Fold top layer edges to meet the middle.

8

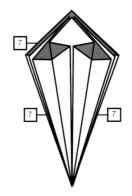

Repeat step 7 to both sides and behind.

9

Fold front petal down.

10

Repeat step 9 on all three sides making the model 3D. Start with both side petals followed by the back petal.

11

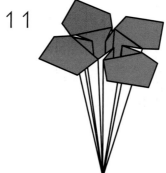

Completed iris.

LILY

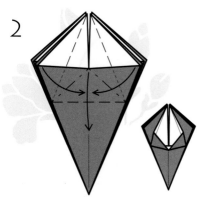

Follow the instructions for the iris on the previous page up to step 7, but start with the colored side up.

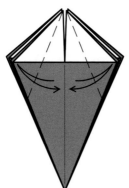

1

Start from step 7 of the iris.
Fold the top layer only to the center crease.

2

Petal fold; pull down the top layer, and fold the sides to the middle. Lastly, make the mountain folds.

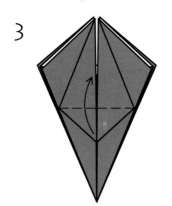

3

Completed petal fold.
Fold the triangle flap upwards.

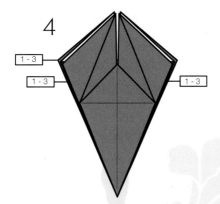

4

1 - 3
1 - 3
1 - 3

Repeat steps 1-3 on the three remaining sides.

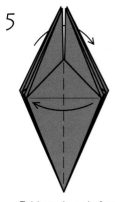

5

Fold one layer in front and behind.

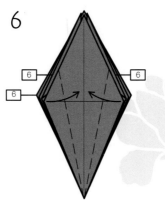

6

6
6
6

Fold edges to the middle, thinning the lily. Repeat on the other three sides.

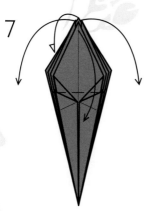

7

Make a soft, curved valley fold on all four sides to open out the lily.

8

Completed lily.

VERDI'S VASE

This traditional Chinese vase was popularized in the United States by Verdi Adams, who taught it to a generation of paperfolders at The Origami Center of America. It is a fantastic model that produces a solid 3D form. Be careful when opening the model during the last steps so the paper doesn't crumple.

These diagrams were originally published in the OUSA Newsletter # 34, Fall 1989. They are reproduced here with permisson from Mark Kennedy.

1 White side up. Crease into sixths in both directions.

2 Crease in half the first, third, fourth and sixth 6ths in both directions.

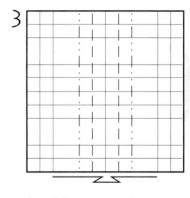

3 On existing creases, pleat to the center line.

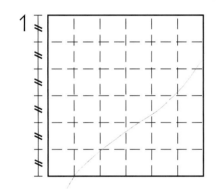

4 On existing creases, pleat to the center line.

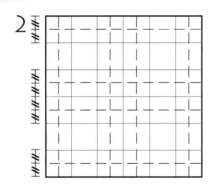

5 The model should look like this. Turn over.

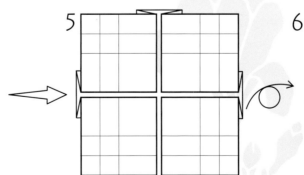

6 Completed step 5.

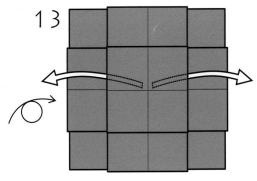

6A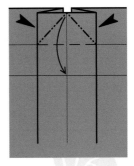

Pull down top layer while squashing in the sides.

6B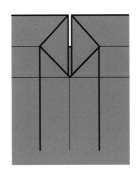

Squashes complete.

7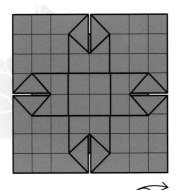

Moves completed on all four sides. Turn over.

8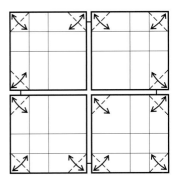

Pre-crease corners as shown to make step 11 easier.

9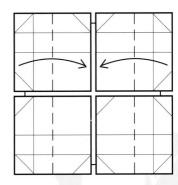

Cupboard door fold sides to the center.

10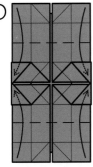

Cupboard door fold top and bottom to center and tuck the corners into the pockets.

11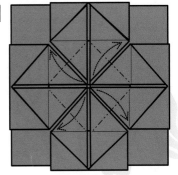

Cupboard door fold top and bottom to center and tuck the corners into the pockets.

12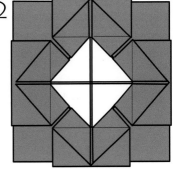

All folding is done. Turn over.

13

Start to open out vase by pulling out the extra layers along the sides. Be careful and work slowly.

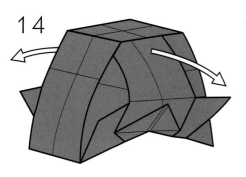

One pair of sides already pulled out. Pull out the other side.

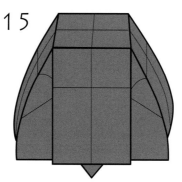

All sides are pulled out.

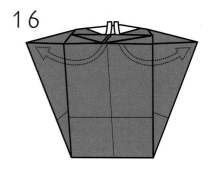

Turn over. Reach inside the top of the vase, poke out and round the corners.

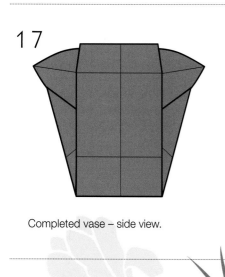

Completed vase – side view.

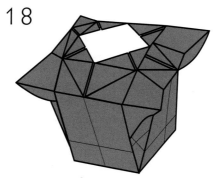

Completed vase – top view.

ALPINE LANDSCAPE

T he Alpine landscape is an innovative decoration by artist Gareth Louis. The final form uses color changes in the paper to show the shadow of a tree in perspective. This model will sit nicely on a desk or mantelpiece as a unique artwork.

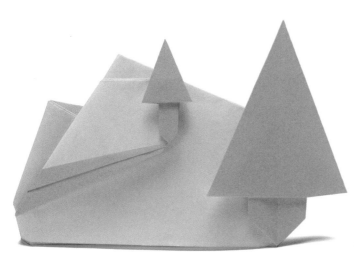

Gareth Louis' origami often has a charming sense of humor, and high degree of practicality.

1

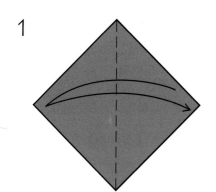

Colored side up. Pre-crease.

2

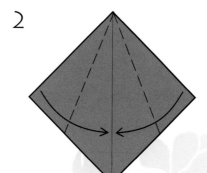

Valley fold raw edges to the center crease.

3

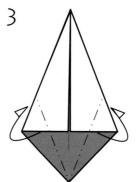

Mountain fold along angle bisectors.

4

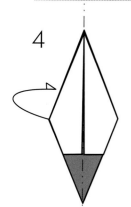

Mountain fold in half.

5

Reverse fold along angle bisectors of the colored region.

6

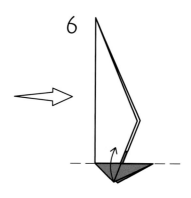

Open up a colored flap.

7

Valley fold.

8

Valley fold arbitrarily.

9

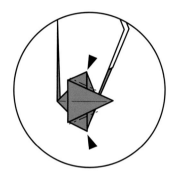

Enlargement. Pre-crease along edges then reverse the two tips.

10

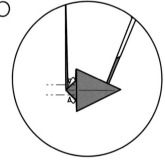

Mountain fold to narrow the stem.

11

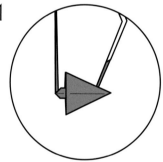

Completed timber.

12

Normal view. Reverse the point arbitrarily.

13

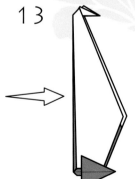

Completed step 12. Turn over.

14

Unfold down.

15

Wrap around a layer to reveal an alternate color.

16

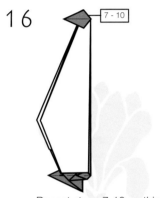

7 - 10

Repeat steps 7-10 on this
colored segment.

17

Mountain fold arbitrarily. Look at the
next drawing for the correct position.
Turn over.

18

Like this.

19

90°

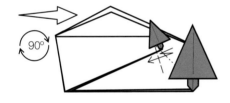

Rotate 90°. Pleat the small tree into
position.

20

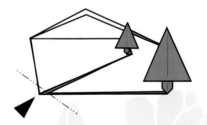

Reverse tip.

21

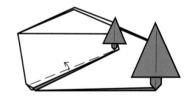

Make a tiny squash releasing a small
portion of trapped paper. Now there
is a little trail.

22

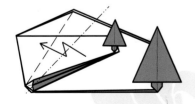

Pleat arbitrarily to form the hills.

23

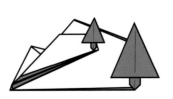

Completed step 22. Turn over.

24

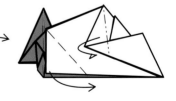

Mountain fold to lock the hills.
Then valley fold outwards lightly...

25

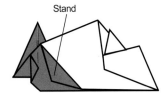

...and you will have a stand for the model. Turn over.

26

To reveal the landscape, shape off any area as you desire.

27

Completed alpine landscape.

PUFFY STAR

T he puffy star is a traditional form popular in Asian countries. It is often made for New Year celebrations for good luck. They can be strung together with a needle and thread to make hanging decorations. You will need strips of paper about 0.6 inch x 12 inches (1.5 cm x 30 cm).

Knotology, a term coined by Heinz Strobl, is the art of folding strips of paper. Many geometric forms can be made from making the pentagon as shown below.

1

Cut 0.6 inch (1.5 cm) from a letter (8.5 x 11 inch) sheet of paper.

2

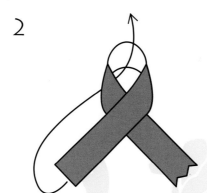

At one end of the strip, make a knot as shown.

3

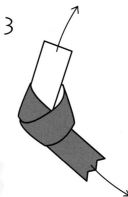

Gently pull both ends until the pentagonal shape is clearly formed.

4

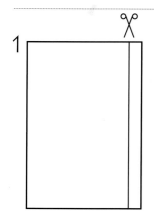

Fold the end of the strip over and tuck under the layer.

5

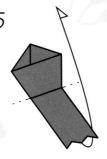

The next steps follow the pentagon shape, wrapping up the puffy star.

6

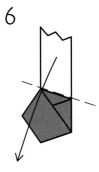

Valley fold.

7

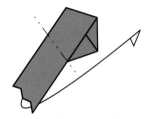

Mountain fold.

8

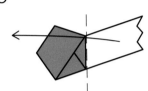

Valley fold.

9

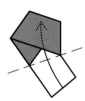

Keep wrapping until you end up with a small stub. Tuck the stub under the next layer.

10

Hold at the circles and use the back of your nail to push in the side of the star.

11

Step 10 completed.

12

Push in the wall of the star on the remaining sides.

13

Completed puffy star.

HEART

This heart can be a folded love letter, or a decoration on the front of a card. Use letter (8.5 x 11 inch) paper.

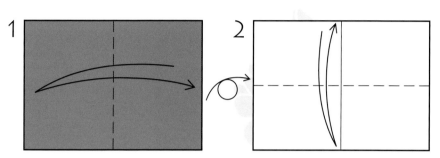

Book fold and unfold. Turn over.

Fold in half lengthways and unfold.

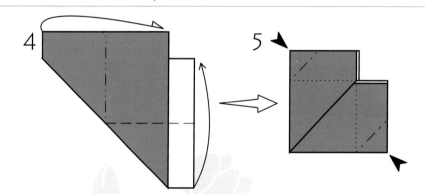

Valley fold a diagonal so that the vertical crease touches the horizontal crease.

Fold the corners together, noting the mountain fold on the upper part and the valley fold on the lower part.

Inside reverse fold the points. The edge of the crease should match with the inner layer of the paper.

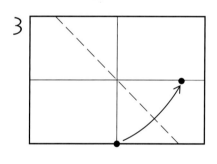

6

7

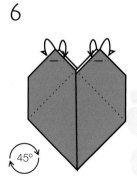

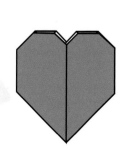

Fold the tips inside the heart.

Completed heart.

Glossary

GEOMETRIC having rectilinear outlines in design

IRIS a purple flower

MANTELPIECE a shelf above a fireplace

PENTAGON a shape with five angles and five sides

PRACTICAL available, usable, or valuable in practice or action

SEQUENCE a continuous or connected series

VARIATION change in the form, position, state, or quality of something

Index

For More Information

Miles, Lisa. *Origami Birds and Butterflies*. New York: Gareth Stevens, 2014.

Owens, Ruth. *More Valentine's Day Origami*. New York: PowerKids Press, 2015.

For web resources related to the subject of this book, go to:
www.windmillbooks.com/weblinks and select this book's title.